ALEX BOLEN

Selling an Inherited Home

A Realtor's Pocket Guide for Selling Your Inherited Home

Contents

1

The Emotional Landscape of Inherited Estates

Selling an inherited estate is a journey unlike any other in the realm of real estate transactions. It's a process that intertwines the practicalities of property sales with the complex and often emotional ties we have to our family homes. My goal is not only to guide you through the logistics of selling your inherited estate but also to help you navigate the unique emotional landscape that accompanies this significant life transition.

The purpose of this book is to provide you with short and concise tips, advice, and knowledge about what occurs behind the scenes and what you can actively do to navigate this often challenging transition smoothly. Feel free to take notes, underline, highlight, and engage with the content on these pages. At the end of each chapter is a summary with bullet points for you to quickly and easily reference in the future so you don't have to re-read the entire chapter for quick tips.

The Layers of Emotion

Inherited homes are repositories of memories – echoes of laughter, the warmth of shared meals, and the comforting familiarity of family traditions. When it comes time to sell, these homes cease to be just structures with walls; they become emotional reservoirs, holding the essence of family history.

The decision to sell an inherited estate is rarely purely financial. It's a multifaceted choice that involves grappling with grief, nostalgia, and the inevitable waves of sentimentality. It's about saying goodbye to more than just a property; it's bidding farewell to a chapter of your life.

As a realtor specializing in historic homes and inherited estates, I've witnessed the delicate balance required to navigate the emotional and practical aspects of this process. It's essential to acknowledge and honor the emotional weight of the home while simultaneously addressing the necessary steps to prepare, market, and sell the property. By understanding and acknowledging these feelings, we can develop strategies to help you move through the process with greater ease and clarity. From the initial decision to sell to the final closing, every step involves a dance between the sentimental and the practical.

The Decision to Sell

The decision to sell an inherited estate is a deeply personal one, often marked by conflicting emotions. Some may feel a sense of duty to maintain the family home, while others might be eager to sever ties and move forward. Recognizing and understanding your emotions is the first step in navigating this intricate terrain.

In the chapters to come, we'll address the practical aspects of selling an inherited estate, but remember this: Your emotions are not secondary to the transaction; they are an integral part of the journey. Together, let's embark on this path with empathy, understanding, and a commitment to honoring the legacy of your family home.

2

Addressing Grief and Sentimentality in Celebrating the Home's Legacy

The sale of an inherited estate is often accompanied by a multitude of emotions, including grief and sentimentality. Together we can explore the process of recognizing and addressing these emotions while celebrating the legacy of the home. By acknowledging the significance of the property's past, you can navigate the sale of an inherited home with compassion, creating a meaningful transition for all involved.

The sale of an inherited home can trigger a grieving process among heirs. Whether it's the loss of a loved one, the end of an era, or the relinquishment of cherished memories, grief can manifest in various forms. Recognizing the journey of grief is essential for approaching the selling process with empathy and understanding.

Below are seven thoughtful approaches to address the emotions of grief and facilitate a smooth transition of ownership to the new proprietors. This process, while ushering in a new chapter for the property, is designed not only to honor the memories held within its walls but also to preserve those recollections for your own heart and the fellow heirs who share this emotional journey with you. These strategies encompass a holistic approach, aiming to weave a tapestry of reflection, commemoration, and the gentle passing of the torch to ensure the home's legacy is carried forward with respect and grace.

1. Create an open and supportive environment for heirs to express their emotions (we'll touch more on communication with heirs in the future). Encourage them to share their memories, thoughts, and feelings associated with the home. A willingness to listen without judgment fosters a sense of validation, allowing heirs to navigate the grieving process while actively participating in the sale.

2. Take the opportunity to memorialize the home's legacy by commemorating significant moments and memories. Consider creating a visual or written tribute that highlights key milestones, events, and the unique features of the property. This commemoration not only acknowledges the home's historical significance but also provides a tangible expression of the cherished memories associated with it.

3. Family stories contribute to the tapestry of a home's history. Incorporate these narratives into the selling process, sharing anecdotes, experiences, and the personal significance of different spaces within the home. Weaving family stories into the sale honors the legacy of the property, creating a connection between the past and the present.

4. Nurture a sense of closure by incorporating personalized farewell rituals. This could include a family gathering, a symbolic ceremony, or the planting of a memorial garden. These rituals provide a structured and meaningful way for heirs to say goodbye, providing a sense of closure and honoring the emotional journey associated with selling the inherited home.

5. Document the home through photography or videography to preserve visual memories. Capture the unique features, architectural details, and significant spaces that hold sentimental value. This documentation serves as a tangible reminder of the home's legacy, allowing heirs to revisit cherished moments even after the sale.

6. Involve heirs in decision-making processes related to the sale, allowing them to contribute to the preservation of the home's legacy. Collaborative decision-making fosters a sense of shared responsibility and ensures that each heir has a role in shaping the narrative of the property's past and its transition to new ownership.

7. Compile a legacy album or book that encapsulates the history of the home. Include photographs, stories, and memorabilia that capture the essence of the property and its role in family history. This keepsake becomes a tangible legacy for heirs, serving as a lasting reminder of the home's significance and the memories it holds.

Navigating grief and sentimentality during the sale of an inherited estate requires a delicate balance of empathy, understanding, and celebration. By acknowledging the complex emotions associated with the home, creating opportunities for expression, and actively commemorating its legacy, you contribute to a meaningful and respectful transition for both heirs and the property itself.

* * *

Chapter 2 Summary:

Recognizing Grief in the Selling Process

- Acknowledge the grieving process triggered by the sale of an inherited home, understanding its various manifestations.

Thoughtful Approaches to Address Grief

1. Create an Open Environment: Encourage heirs to express emotions and memories freely.
2. Memorialize the Home's Legacy: Commemorate significant moments through visual or written tributes.
3. Incorporate Family Stories: Share anecdotes, experiences, and the personal significance of spaces within the home.
4. Personalized Farewell Rituals: Foster closure through symbolic ceremonies or family gatherings.
5. Document the Home: Preserve visual memories through photography or videography.
6. Involve Heirs in Decision-Making: Collaborative decision-making ensures shared responsibility in shaping the property's narrative.

7. Compile a Legacy Album: Create a lasting reminder of the home's significance with a collection of photographs, stories, and memorabilia.

3

Navigating Probate and Legal Processes

The process of selling an inherited estate often involves navigating through probate and legal intricacies. Understanding these legal processes is crucial for a smooth and successful transition. This chapter provides a comprehensive guide to probate, legal considerations, and the steps involved in ensuring that the estate is handled in accordance with legal requirements.

If you've already been through the probate process then this chapter may not be something you need to read up on. If so, feel free to skip to the next to learn about communication with heirs.

Probate

So what is probate? I know before getting into real estate I heard the term thrown around quite a bit but never fully understood what it entailed. Let's dive into it and get a better understanding of what it is, and what you can expect when going through the process.

Probate is the legal process that happens after someone passes away, where their belongings and property are taken care of and given to their heirs. This process involves making sure the person's will, if they have one, is valid and following the laws that apply. The main goals of probate are to settle any debts the person had, give their belongings to the people they wanted, and transfer any property legally.

The probate process usually starts by submitting a request to the court. This kicks off the legal steps to check the person's will and appoint someone called an executor or administrator, to handle the estate. This person has the legal power to manage and distribute the person's belongings. They have a fiduciary relationship, meaning they must act in the best interests of the estate and its beneficiaries.

Getting help from a knowledgeable probate professional, like a probate attorney, can be incredibly helpful. They know the ins and outs of the law and can guide the heirs through the legal processes involved in validating a will, paying off debts, and distributing assets, including real estate.

If the home is in a trust, things might be simpler. Trust-held properties often go through a quicker process because they are already set to go to specific beneficiaries without needing a lot of court involvement. But even in these cases, having a probate attorney to guide through the specific steps is crucial for a smooth and legally sound transition.

When someone has a valid will, the court checks it to make sure it's real and legal. This includes presenting the will to the court with witness testimonies and other needed documents. Once the court says it's valid, the executor can follow the person's wishes.

During probate, the executor or administrator must tell the

deceased person's creditors about their passing. Creditors can file claims for any money owed. The executor reviews these claims, pays valid debts using estate funds, and disputes any claims that are not valid. Once debts are settled, the remaining assets are given to the heirs or beneficiaries according to the will or state laws if there is no will. The executor makes sure everyone gets what they are supposed to.

After finishing all the tasks, the executor asks the court to close the estate. This involves showing all the transactions and distributions made during probate. The court checks everything, makes sure all the legal rules were followed, and officially closes the probate proceedings. With the court's approval, the executor's job is done.

Sometimes, probate can have challenges, like arguments between heirs, disagreements about the will, or disputes with creditors. Resolving these issues might need more court actions, like hearings and discussions. It's a good idea to get legal advice in these situations to handle them correctly.

Knowing the potential challenges of probate, people might explore ways to make the process easier, like making a living trust, naming beneficiaries on financial accounts, or using other strategies to transfer assets efficiently without a lot of probate involvement. By being careful and seeking professional advice when needed, individuals can make sure the transition is legal and smooth, following the wishes outlined in the person's documents and keeping the estate intact.

Pro Tip: Mitigating Probate Challenges Through Estate Planning

While navigating the probate process is often inevitable, individuals can proactively minimize potential challenges in the future through strategic estate planning. Consider implementing the following measures:

Establishing a Living Trust: Creating a living trust allows for the seamless transfer of assets without extensive probate involvement. Assets placed in the trust can pass directly to beneficiaries, expediting the distribution process.

Designating Beneficiaries: Clearly designate beneficiaries on financial accounts, retirement plans, and life insurance policies. This ensures that these assets transfer directly to the intended recipients, bypassing probate complexities.

Regularly Updating Estate Plans: Periodically review and update estate plans to reflect any changes in assets, family structure, or personal preferences. Keeping documents current contributes to a more efficient probate process.

Consulting with Estate Planning Professionals: Seek guidance from estate planning professionals, including attorneys and financial advisors, to develop a comprehensive plan tailored to your specific circumstances. Their expertise can help navigate legal intricacies and minimize potential challenges.

By incorporating these proactive measures into your estate planning strategy, you can mitigate the impact of probate challenges, streamline the transition of assets, and ensure a more efficient and less burdensome process for your heirs.

* * *

Chapter 3 Summary:

Understanding Probate:

- Probate is the legal process through which a deceased person's estate is settled and assets are distributed. It involves validating the will, if one exists, and administering the estate in accordance with applicable laws.

Goals of Probate:

- The primary goals include resolving outstanding debts, distributing assets to heirs, and ensuring the lawful transfer of property.

Engaging Probate Professionals:

- Hiring an experienced probate attorney can provide crucial guidance in navigating the complexities of the probate process, validating the will, settling debts, and distributing assets.

Trust-Held Properties:

- If the home is held within a trust, the probate process can be more streamlined, expediting the distribution process for a more efficient experience.

Executor's Responsibilities:

- The appointed executor or administrator manages the estate, settles debts, compiles an inventory of assets, and notifies creditors.

Dealing with Creditors:

- Creditors are given an opportunity to file claims against the estate, which the executor reviews, pays valid debts, and disputes any deemed invalid.

Asset Distribution:

- After settling debts, remaining assets are distributed to heirs according to the will or state intestacy laws, overseen by the executor or administrator.

Closing the Estate:

- The executor or administrator petitions the court to close the estate, submitting a final accounting for court review and approval.

Potential Challenges:

- Probate proceedings may encounter challenges, requiring additional court proceedings. Seeking legal counsel is advisable to navigate complexities and ensure a fair resolution.

4

Effective Communication with Heirs

Effective communication is the cornerstone of a successful estate transaction, especially when dealing with heirs. Let's delve into the art of navigating conversations with heirs, emphasizing clarity, empathy, and transparency. Understanding the dynamics of these interactions is essential for fostering trust, managing expectations, and ensuring a collaborative and harmonious process.

It is important to recognize that the sale of an inherited estate can evoke a range of emotions among heirs. Sensitivity to the emotional impact of this process is crucial. Begin conversations with an acknowledgment of the emotional aspects involved, expressing empathy for the challenges and sentiments that may arise. By doing this, you create a foundation for open and understanding communication.

From the beginning, establish open lines of communication with heirs. Clearly communicate your availability and preferred methods of communication. Whether through email, phone calls, or in-person meetings, fostering accessibility sets the tone for ongoing dialogue. Encourage heirs to reach out with questions or concerns, emphasizing a collaborative approach throughout the estate transaction.

Transparency is paramount in estate transactions. Provide clear and concise information about the process, timelines, and potential challenges. Avoid jargon and legalese, ensuring that heirs can easily comprehend the details. Transparency builds trust and helps manage expectations, reducing the likelihood of misunderstandings and fostering a collaborative environment.

Heirs may have concerns, questions, or uncertainties about the estate transaction. It is important to practice active listening, allowing them to express their thoughts and feelings. Be sure to demonstrate genuine interest in their perspectives and concerns. Respond thoughtfully and empathetically, addressing each question with clarity. By practicing these tactics we can create a supportive atmosphere that reinforces a sense of collaboration.

Next, it is important to recognize that each heir may have a unique communication style and preferences. Practice tailoring your approach to accommodate these individual needs. Some heirs may prefer detailed written updates, while others may prefer brief verbal summaries. Understanding and adapting to diverse communication styles contribute to effective interactions with heirs.

Along with understanding communication styles, timely communication is essential for keeping heirs informed throughout the estate transaction. Provide regular updates on the progress of the sale, key milestones, and any changes in the process. Even if there are no significant developments, a brief update can reassure heirs and demonstrate your commitment to transparency and communication.

A good way to stay on top of things is by anticipating common questions and concerns that heirs may have during the estate transaction. By proactively addressing these issues in your communication you can provide information that alleviates potential worries and contribute to a smoother and more collaborative process.

Effective communication also involves setting realistic expectations. Clearly articulate the anticipated timelines, potential challenges, and any uncertainties in the process. Managing heirs' expectations prevents disappointments and frustrations, building a collaborative atmosphere based on trust and transparency.

I would recommend facilitating family meetings, either in person or virtually, to encourage open dialogue among heirs. Family meetings provide an opportunity for everyone to express their thoughts, share concerns, and collectively discuss decisions related to the estate. Facilitating a collaborative environment through family meetings contributes to a smoother decision-making process.

In complex estate transactions, visual aids can greatly enhance clarity and understanding. Consider using charts, graphs, or timelines to illustrate key points and processes. Visual aids simplify complex information, making it more accessible to heirs and reinforcing your commitment to transparent communication.

In conclusion, effective communication with heirs is an integral aspect of successful estate transactions. By acknowledging sensitivities, establishing accessibility, providing transparent information, and customizing communication styles, you build trust and collaboration. Proactive communication, timely updates, and a focus on managing expectations contribute to a positive and fruitful experience for all parties involved in the estate transaction.

Pro Tip: Leveraging Video Communication

Incorporate video messages into your communication strategy with heirs. While written updates and phone calls are valuable, a personalized video can add a human touch to your interactions. You can use brief video updates to share progress, discuss key milestones, or address any concerns. This visual communication not only provides a more personal connection but also allows heirs to see your sincerity and commitment. Keep the videos concise and focused, creating a sense of transparency and accessibility. This innovative approach can strengthen the bond between you and the heirs, fostering a deeper understanding and collaboration throughout the estate transaction.

* * *

Chapter 4 Summary:

Sensitivity to Emotions

- Acknowledge the emotional impact of selling an inherited estate, setting the foundation for open and understanding communication.

Establish Open Communication

- Clearly convey your availability and preferred communication methods to foster ongoing dialogue with heirs.

Transparency is Key

- Provide clear and concise information about the estate transaction, avoiding jargon, and ensuring easy comprehension.

Active Listening

- Practice active listening to address concerns, allowing heirs to express thoughts and feelings freely.

Tailor Communication Styles

- Recognize and adapt to each heir's unique communication style and preferences for a more personalized approach.

Timely Updates

- Regularly communicate updates on the sale's progress, key milestones, and any changes, maintaining transparency and reassurance.

Proactive Problem-Solving

· Anticipate and address common questions and concerns, contributing to a smoother and more collaborative process.

Realistic Expectations

· Set realistic expectations by clearly articulating anticipated timelines, potential challenges, and uncertainties.

Family Meetings

· Consider facilitating family meetings to encourage open dialogue, collaboration, and collective decision-making.

Visual Aids for Clarity

· Use visual aids, such as charts or timelines, to enhance understanding in complex estate transactions.

5

Selecting the Ideal Guide

In the intricate process of selling an inherited estate, the choice of a realtor holds unparalleled significance. Dealing with the complexities of inherited properties demands a realtor possessing specific traits and expertise. This chapter explores the crucial qualities to seek in a realtor, emphasizing the nuanced challenges inherent in handling inherited estates.

Firstly, if possible, look for a realtor with specialized experience in inherited estates. Proficiency in probate, legal considerations, and an understanding of the emotional nuances associated with selling an inherited property is vital. Such expertise positions the realtor to provide valuable insights, minimizing potential complications and facilitating a seamless process. A realtor with heightened sensitivity and empathy comprehends the unique challenges faced by individuals in these circumstances. By approaching the process with compassion, they offer support and guidance while acknowledging and respecting the emotional aspects that accompany the sale.

Everything starts with effective communication, which forms the bedrock of a successful real estate transaction. Seek a realtor who communicates with clarity and consistency. Keeping you informed at every stage, explaining complex terms in accessible language, and being readily available for your questions and concerns establishes a foundation of trust and ensures a collaborative and transparent selling experience.

Where are you selling? Where is your realtor located? A realtor's in-depth knowledge of the local real estate market is indispensable. Familiarity with property values, market trends, and neighborhood dynamics allows the realtor to accurately price the inherited estate, devise effective marketing strategies, and negotiate advantageous terms. Look for a realtor with insights specific to the area where the property is located.

Let's also consider their network. A well-connected realtor with a robust professional network is a valuable asset, particularly in the context of inherited estates. Their access to a team of professionals, including probate attorneys, appraisers, inspectors, and other experts, ensures a streamlined process. The realtor orchestrates a cohesive team to address the legal, financial, and logistical aspects of the sale.

Estates may present unforeseen challenges, requiring a realtor with a proactive problem-solving approach. Seek someone capable of anticipating potential issues, developing contingency plans, and navigating obstacles with ease. Their ability to think ahead and address challenges as they arise contributes to a smoother and more resilient selling process.

Integrity is non-negotiable in a realtor, in fact it is their duty thanks to the realtor code of ethics. Seek someone who conducts business with transparency, honesty, and ethical standards. A realtor with integrity prioritizes your best interests, discloses relevant information, and operates within legal and ethical guidelines. Just like we discussed earlier with executor's having a fiduciary relationship with the estate & heirs, realtors have this same fiduciary relationship with their clients. This ensures a trustworthy partnership throughout the entire real estate transaction.

Next, let's consider how they are going to market your property. Effective marketing is crucial in attracting potential buyers, and a realtor with strong marketing expertise can make a significant difference. Seek someone with a comprehensive marketing plan that leverages various channels, including online platforms, traditional media, and networking groups and events. A well-executed marketing strategy enhances the property's visibility and accelerates the selling process.

After marketing comes negotiation. Negotiation is central to real estate transactions, making strong negotiation skills a critical asset. Seek a realtor who demonstrates proficiency in securing the best possible price, navigating inspection-related negotiations, and addressing contingencies. Their ability to advocate for your interests ensures a favorable and equitable deal.

Lastly, and possibly most importantly, seek a realtor who understands your unique circumstances, goals, and priorities, customizing their services to meet your specific needs. A realtor who prioritizes your objectives ensures that the selling process aligns with your expectations and delivers a positive outcome. Especially when dealing with inherited homes, money isn't always everyone's main goal, there are many factors that surround estates that make other things such as smooth and easy transactions paramount.

Pro Tip: SRES® Designation

Consider the added benefit of finding a realtor with the Seniors Real Estate Specialist (SRES®) designation. Realtors with this designation have received specialized training to address the unique needs and challenges of clients aged 50 and older. Their expertise includes understanding the financial and emotional components of selling an inherited estate, making them well-suited to navigate the complexities involved.

Choosing the right realtor for selling an inherited estate is a pivotal decision with far-reaching implications. By prioritizing these essential qualities and considering the specialized expertise denoted by the SRES® designation, you ensure that your realtor possesses the necessary skills and insight to guide you through the intricate landscape of selling an inherited property, ultimately leading to a successful and well-managed transaction.

* * *

Chapter 5 Summary:

Realtor's Significance

- Crucial choice in the complex process of selling an inherited estate.
- Demands specific traits and expertise due to the intricacies of inherited properties.

Specialized Experience

- Seek a realtor experienced in inherited estates.
- Proficiency in probate, legal considerations, and under-standing emotional nuances is vital.
- Offers valuable insights, minimizes complications, and facilitates a seamless process.

Sensitivity and Empathy

- Look for a realtor with heightened sensitivity and empathy.
- Comprehends unique challenges, provides support, and respects emotional aspects.

Effective Communication

- Communication with clarity and consistency is essential.
- Keeps you informed, explains complex terms, and is readily

available.
- Establishes trust, ensuring a collaborative and transparent selling experience.

Local Knowledge

- In-depth knowledge of the local real estate market is indispensable.
- Facilitates accurate pricing, effective marketing, and negotiation advantage.

Professional Network

- Well-connected realtor with a robust professional network is valuable.
- Access to a team of professionals ensures a streamlined process.

Problem-Solving Skills

- Seek a realtor with proactive problem-solving skills.
- Anticipates potential issues, develops contingency plans, and navigates obstacles.

Integrity

- Non-negotiable quality in a realtor.

- Conducts business with transparency, honesty, and ethical standards.

Marketing Expertise

- Effective marketing is crucial.
- Seek a realtor with a comprehensive marketing plan leveraging various channels.

Negotiation Skills

- Strong negotiation skills are critical.
- Proficient in securing the best possible price and addressing contingencies.

Client-Centric Approach

- Prioritizes your unique circumstances, goals, and priorities.
- Customizes services to meet your specific needs, ensuring a positive outcome.

6

Preparing to Sell: Assessing Your Inherited Estate

Before diving into the complexities of selling your inherited estate, it's crucial to assess the property's condition thoroughly. This chapter will guide you through the process of evaluating your estate's physical state, considering factors that may affect its market value, and making informed decisions to enhance its appeal to potential buyers. If you are working with a realtor, they will help you with this process and highlight any problem areas with your inherited estate that may be worth fixing prior to selling.

Upon inheriting a property, sellers often face the challenge of understanding its true condition. Beyond the sentimental value, it's essential to objectively evaluate the structural integrity, functionality of systems, and overall livability. This evaluation becomes particularly vital when the seller may not be well-versed in home maintenance or if the property has been vacant.

1. **Exterior Evaluation:**

- Begin by assessing the exterior of the property. Look for signs of wear and tear, such as damaged siding, roofing issues, or overgrown landscaping.
- Curb appeal plays a significant role in creating a positive first impression for potential buyers.

2. **Interior Inspection:**

- Conduct a thorough inspection of the interior spaces. Pay attention to the condition of walls, flooring, and ceilings.
- Check for any potential structural issues, water damage, or the need for cosmetic improvements.

3. **Systems and Appliances:**

- Evaluate the functionality of key systems such as plumbing, electrical, and heating/cooling.
- Assess the condition of appliances that may be included in the sale, providing potential buyers with confidence in the property's overall livability.

Understanding the Importance of a Home Inspector

For sellers who may not have an in-depth understanding of home structures and systems, hiring a home inspector can be a strategic move. A home inspector is a trained professional who assesses the condition of a property, identifying potential issues that may not be immediately apparent. Their expertise can be especially beneficial when selling an inherited estate, where the seller might not be familiar with the property's history or potential hidden problems. Home inspectors provide an unbiased and impartial assessment of the property's condition, offering insights that go beyond the surface appearance.

Upon completion of the inspection you will receive a comprehensive report detailing the property's current state, highlighting any areas of immediate concern, and offering suggestions for improvements. This information not only equips sellers with a clearer understanding of their property's condition but also allows them to address critical issues proactively.

An inspector's expertise extends to identifying hidden issues that may not be evident during a casual walkthrough. Sellers benefit from this thorough examination, as it enables them to address concerns before listing the property. By tackling potential problems proactively, sellers can enhance the overall appeal of their inherited estate in the competitive real estate market.

If you feel emotionally attached to your home and don't know much about its maintenance history, hiring an inspector before selling can be an invaluable asset.

Prioritization of Repairs and Enhanced Buyer Confidence

Beyond identifying issues, home inspectors and realtors play a pivotal role in helping sellers prioritize repairs or improvements based on urgency and potential impact on the property's value. This strategic approach empowers sellers to make informed decisions, allocating resources where they matter most.

Furthermore, the insights provided by a home inspector can be shared transparently with potential buyers. This transparency not only enhances buyer confidence but also demonstrates the seller's commitment to honesty and integrity throughout the selling process. Providing a home inspection report becomes a valuable tool in showcasing the property's condition and addressing any concerns upfront.

The Emotional and Practical Benefits of an Estate Sale

Undertaking the sale of an inherited estate often comes with the emotional challenge of parting with cherished belongings and memories. One impactful strategy to ease this process is considering an estate sale as part of your pre-sale preparations. An estate sale not only provides a practical means of decluttering and preparing the property for listing but also serves as a therapeutic avenue for overcoming emotional difficulties. Sorting through possessions, deciding what to keep, and what to part with can be emotionally taxing. To ease this burden, consider involving family members in the process and reminiscing about shared memories.

I'd encourage you to embrace the idea that passing on belongings to new owners ensures they continue to be cherished in new homes. Collaborating with a professional estate sale organizer can also alleviate the logistical challenges, leaving you with a streamlined and organized property ready for potential buyers, allowing both the emotional and practical aspects of the selling process to harmoniously coexist.

Should you handle the estate sale yourself or hire an expert? Handling the estate sale personally provides an intimate connection with the process. It allows for a more hands-on approach, providing an opportunity to reminisce about cherished memories associated with each item. Additionally, managing the sale personally may result in a more significant financial return, as you have direct control over pricing and negotiations. On the flip side, managing the estate sale personally can be emotionally taxing and time-consuming. The process may dredge up memories, making it challenging to detach emotionally from certain items. Logistics, such as advertising the sale, managing inquiries, and overseeing transactions, can become overwhelming, potentially prolonging the emotional strain.

Enlisting the services of a professional estate sale organizer offers numerous advantages. These experts bring a wealth of experience, streamlining the process with efficiency. They possess a keen understanding of market values, ensuring items are priced competitively. A professional organizer can manage the logistical aspects, from advertising the sale to handling transactions, alleviating the burden on the seller. This allows you to focus on the emotional transition, knowing that the practical aspects are in capable hands.

While hiring a professional estate organizer can simplify the process, it does come with associated costs. Fees for their services, typically a percentage of the total sale, should be factored into the overall budget.

* * *

Chapter 6 Summary:

Crucial Preliminary Assessment

- Thoroughly assess the property's condition before delving into the complexities of selling the inherited estate.
- Objective evaluation is essential beyond sentimental value, focusing on structural integrity, system functionality, and overall livability.

Exterior Evaluation

- Check the exterior for signs of wear and tear.
- Evaluate landscaping and address any issues to enhance curb appeal, leaving a positive first impression for potential buyers.

Interior Inspection

- Conduct a comprehensive inspection of interior spaces.
- Pay attention to the condition of walls, flooring, and ceilings.
- Identify potential structural issues, water damage, or the need for cosmetic improvements.

Systems and Appliances Evaluation

- Assess the functionality of key systems: plumbing, electrical, heating/cooling.
- Examine the condition of appliances included in the sale, instilling confidence in the property's overall livability.

Understanding the Importance of a Home Inspector

- For sellers less familiar with home maintenance, hiring a home inspector is strategic.
- Home inspectors provide a comprehensive report on the property's condition, revealing hidden issues and suggesting improvements.
- Objective evaluation and impartial assessment contribute to a deeper understanding of the property's state.

Advantages of a Home Inspector

- Identify hidden issues not evident during a casual walk-through.
- Enable proactive addressing of concerns before listing the property.
- Particularly crucial for inherited properties due to potential emotional attachment and lack of familiarity with the home's history.

Prioritization of Repairs and Enhanced Buyer Confidence

- Home inspectors help sellers prioritize repairs based on

urgency and potential impact on property value.

- Empower sellers to make informed decisions and allocate resources strategically.
- Insights from a home inspector can be shared transparently with potential buyers, enhancing buyer confidence and showcasing the property's condition.
- Providing a home inspection report demonstrates the seller's commitment to honesty and integrity throughout the selling process.

Estate Sale as a Strategy

- Consider an estate sale as part of pre-sale preparations for emotional and practical benefits.

Decluttering and Emotional Process

- Estate sales offer a practical means of decluttering while providing a therapeutic avenue for overcoming emotional challenges associated with parting with cherished belongings and memories.

Involvement of Family Members

- Involve family members in the process to ease the emotional burden, reminiscing about shared memories.

Passing on Belongings

- Embrace the idea that passing on belongings to new owners ensures they continue to be cherished in new homes.

Professional Estate Sale Organizer

- Collaborating with a professional estate sale organizer can alleviate logistical challenges, leaving you with a stream-lined and organized property.

Handling Personally

- Handling the estate sale personally provides an intimate connection with the process, allowing for a hands-on approach and potentially a more significant financial return.

7

Setting the Stage: Realistic Pricing for Your Inherited Estate

Now that you've assessed your property and prepared it for the sale, you're at the pivotal task of determining the asking price. Setting a realistic price involves a balance between emotional attachment, market realities, and the unique features of your property. In this chapter, we'll explore the considerations that go into establishing an asking price that not only reflects the market value but also resonates with potential buyers.

Navigating the intricacies of pricing an inherited estate can be a complex endeavor, but a skilled realtor is your ally in this process. Their expertise and understanding of the local market are invaluable. By engaging with a realtor, you can leverage their insights into current market trends, receive guidance on comparable sales, and benefit from their ability to objectively assess your property's condition.

Sellers of inherited estates often find themselves wrestling with the emotional ties to their property. The memories and sentimental value associated with the home can significantly influence their perception of its worth. However, it's crucial to recognize that the market value is determined by various factors, including location, comparable sales, and current market conditions and any emotional ties to the property do not add to its market market value.

When deciding on the price for your inherited property, it's crucial to do market research. This involves looking at recently sold properties in your area that are similar to yours, often called "comps." These comparable sales give you a realistic idea of the market value by considering factors like the number of bedrooms and bathrooms, as well as the architectural style. Analyzing comps helps you set a competitive and market-driven price for your property.

It's essential to recognize that no two properties are identical, and adjustments may be needed to account for variations. Factors like upgrades, additional features, or unique characteristics that differentiate your property from selected comps should be carefully evaluated.

Using insights from comparable sales, you and your realtor can determine a competitive and fair asking price. This well-researched price not only attracts potential buyers but also minimizes the risk of overpricing, which can deter interest.

Assessing whether you are in a seller's market or a buyer's market is also crucial. In a seller's market, where demand exceeds supply, you may have more flexibility in setting a slightly higher price. Conversely, in a buyer's market, a more competitive approach may be necessary. Staying informed about economic factors such as interest rates, job growth, and regional economic stability is also paramount, as these factors can influence buyer behavior.

Trends in property values should be tracked to anticipate potential fluctuations. Knowing whether values are increasing, decreasing, or stabilizing provides valuable context for pricing decisions.

Pro Tip: Strategic Timing for Maximum Impact

Consider the timing of your listing strategically. Research shows that the time of year can impact the real estate market. Spring and early summer are often considered prime seasons, with increased buyer activity. However, listing during the off-season might yield less competition, potentially attracting more serious buyers. Keep in mind that sometimes, personal circumstances may necessitate a sale regardless of the season. Discuss the optimal timing with your realtor to align your listing with market dynamics for maximum impact and a more successful sale.

* * *

Chapter 7 Summary:

Determining the Asking Price

- The critical task of selling your inherited estate begins with setting a realistic asking price, balancing emotional attachment, market realities, and unique property features.

Realtor as Your Guide

- A skilled realtor is essential in navigating the complexities of pricing. Their expertise, local market understanding, and objective property assessment are invaluable.

Emotional Ties and Market Value

- Sellers often grapple with emotional ties influencing their perceived property worth. Market value, however, is determined by factors like location, comparable sales, and current market conditions.

Market Research Fundamentals

- Thorough market research, examining recent sales of similar properties, is fundamental. Open communication with a realtor provides insights into local market trends, buyer expectations, and pricing factors.

Role of Comparable Sales (Comps)

- Analyzing comparable sales (comps) establishes a benchmark for a competitive and market-driven price. Collaborating with your realtor, select relevant comps based on size, condition, and amenities.

Avoiding Overpricing

- Using insights from comps, determine a competitive and fair asking price to attract potential buyers and minimize the risk of overpricing, which can deter interest.

Adapting to Market Environment

- Understanding the current market environment is crucial. A realtor, equipped with the latest market data, guides you in making informed decisions and adjusting your approach to align with buyer expectations.

Seller's vs. Buyer's Market

- Assessing whether you are in a seller's or buyer's market is crucial for setting the right price. Economic factors such as interest rates, job growth, and regional stability impact buyer behavior.

Tracking Property Value Trends

- Regularly track trends in property values to anticipate potential fluctuations. Knowing whether values are increasing, decreasing, or stabilizing provides valuable context for pricing decisions.

8

Showcasing Your Inherited Estate: Effective Marketing Strategies

Now that you've set a realistic asking price, the next crucial step is to effectively market your inherited estate to potential buyers. This chapter explores strategies to highlight the unique features of your property, create a compelling narrative, and ultimately capture the attention of those in the market for a new home.

In the world of real estate, first impressions matter. A well-presented property not only enhances its appeal but also attracts a wider audience. Invest in professional photography to capture high-resolution images that showcase the details of your home. Services like these are usually covered by a realtor, but if you're listing by yourself this is an absolute must. Additionally, staging your inherited estate can create a welcoming atmosphere, helping potential buyers envision the potential of each space.

Your property listing is the virtual introduction to potential buyers. Collaborate with your realtor to create a listing that effectively communicates the unique selling points of your inherited estate. Craft compelling and engaging property descriptions that use descriptive language to evoke emotions. Highlight any unique features that set your property apart and provide clear and comprehensive information about the home. The description is a great place to also talk about any upgrades you've recently made to the home after inheriting it. Major appliances and roofs are main concerns for buyers as they are the most costly, so if you can add "New roof, new water heater, etc." it is a big weight off of potential buyers shoulders. In this day and age using AI tools to generate well written listing descriptions is lucrative. Not only does it save you time, but it can compile everything you want to communicate about the home thoughtfully and succinctly.

If you've hired a realtor, they will take the lead on crafting a compelling listing and managing the marketing efforts. Realtors have access to professional networks, marketing resources, and industry expertise to effectively promote your property. However, there are still ways you can contribute to the marketing process such as sharing the listing online through social media and raising awareness to neighbors that the home is for sale. A lot of times neighbors bring buyers to the table as they may know people that are looking to buy in the area.

While online platforms for marketing your home are essential, in-person experiences remain pivotal in the home-buying process. Organize open houses and private showings to give potential buyers a firsthand look at the property. Host open house events to attract a diverse range of potential buyers and create a welcoming atmosphere. Accommodate private showings by appointment to offer a personalized experience, allowing potential buyers to explore the property at their own pace. The nice thing about inherited homes is that you most likely aren't living there, so showing accommodations can be made hassle free by your realtor with automatic confirmations.

The real estate market is dynamic, and flexibility is key. Work closely with your realtor to adapt your marketing strategies based on feedback, market trends, and the evolving needs of potential buyers. A realtor will provide valuable insights and guide you in adjusting your approach to maximize your property's visibility and appeal.

Pro Tip: Harness the Power of Social Media

Make sure you maximize the potential of social media platforms to promote your listing. You can do this by utilizing visually attractive content, including high-quality images and videos, on platforms such as Instagram and Facebook. Craft compelling posts that narrate the unique history and features of your property. Consider sharing these posts in local neighborhood groups to enhance visibility and encourage neighbors to spread the word about the sale. Collaborate with your realtor to incorporate social media marketing into their overall strategy, broadening the reach and generating increased interest in your inherited estate.

* * *

Chapter 8 Summary:

Hire Professionals

- Enhance the appeal of your inherited estate with professional photography and staging.

Highlight what Makes it Unique

- Craft a compelling property listing with your realtor, emphasizing unique features and recent upgrades.

Take Advantage of Networks

- Utilize your realtor's professional networks and marketing resources for effective promotion.

In-Person Experiences

- Organize open houses and private showings to provide in-person experiences for potential buyers.

Use Social Media

- Harness the power of social media to reach a broader audience and generate interest in your property.

9

The Art of Closing the Deal

As prospective buyers express interest and offers start to roll in, entering the negotiation phase is a critical step in selling your inherited estate. Navigating negotiations requires a balance of assertiveness, flexibility, and a keen understanding of market dynamics. Here, we explore the nuances of this stage in the selling process and offer insights into maximizing value while ensuring a smooth and successful transaction.

As negotiations unfold, delving into the buyer's perspective is absolutely essential. Buyers, motivated by a desire to secure a favorable deal, often scrutinize every aspect of a property, identifying potential issues as leverage for negotiating a lower price. Recognizing that buyers are inherently seeking value, sellers should be mindful of the fact that they may perceive certain aspects of the property as opportunities for a discounted offer.

Understanding this dynamic enables sellers to anticipate potential negotiation points and engage in discussions with a strategic awareness of the buyer's intentions. While sellers focus on showcasing the positive aspects of their inherited estate, the realtor plays an important role in deciphering and addressing the buyer's motivations, facilitating a more informed and effective negotiation process.

Negotiations thrive on realistic expectations. While every seller desires the highest possible offer, setting expectations grounded in market realities is crucial. Sellers should focus on their financial goals and priorities, understanding that their realtor, armed with market expertise, provides insights into comparable sales, current market conditions, and the buyer's financial position. This information empowers sellers to make informed decisions, balancing financial objectives with the realities of the market.

Flexibility is another valuable asset in negotiations, and sellers should be open to compromises on certain terms to facilitate a smoother process. Considerations such as closing dates, potential repairs, or adjustments in the sale price may require a flexible approach and should be considered. Sellers can strategically leverage flexibility to find common ground, fostering a positive negotiating atmosphere.

With all these tips in your bag, it's important to recognize that negotiations can be time-consuming, requiring patience from all parties involved. Sellers should understand that both buyers and sellers may need time to assess and respond to offers. Patience allows for thoughtful consideration of terms, reducing the likelihood of rushed decisions that could impact the overall success of the transaction. In addition to patience, remember that if you are working with other heirs on the sale of your inherited home, offers will need to be considered by all heirs that hold interest. While sellers exercise patience, realtors manage timelines, ensuring that the negotiation process progresses efficiently and effectively.

Navigating the Inspection Process as a Seller

As your inherited property progresses through the selling journey, the inspection phase emerges as a critical step once the home is under contract. Recognizing the purpose of inspections as a standard practice in real estate transactions sets the stage for a collaborative approach to this pivotal step.

Inspections take place as outlined in the purchase agreement. Sometimes buyers will choose to waive inspections, which means that they forfeit their opportunity to conduct an assessment of the property and back out of the deal scotch free if they find anything not up to snuff. Most of the time buyers will have 5-10 days from the effective date of the purchase agreement to conduct inspections. They will then have the opportunity to proceed with the sale, back out of the sale, or renegotiate the terms of the sale. This inspection period usually involves the buyers hiring an inspector to conduct the inspections, but can also include others as they gather quotes for anything they may need repaired.

Preparation by the sellers is crucial for a successful inspection. Make sure you proactively address any issues based on earlier evaluations or recommendations from a home inspector prior to listing the home, or if you're selling the home "as-is" be prepared for the buyer to make some discoveries they weren't originally expecting and want to renegotiate.

On the inspection day, let the buyer and inspector have space to conduct the inspection without your interference. This is often a safe space for buyers to talk confidentially with their realtor and inspector about any concerns they have. You want the buyer to be able to feel safe and not burdened by your presence. Ensure the property is neat and accessible, reflecting positively on its overall maintenance and contributing to a smoother inspection process.

Upon completion of the inspection, the buyers will receive a detailed report outlining findings related to structural elements, systems, appliances, and potential areas of concern. The report may indicate no significant issues, minor concerns, or major findings, each requiring a unique approach to negotiations and determining the next steps.

Approach negotiations collaboratively, acknowledging reasonable concerns raised by the buyer. Prioritize repairs based on their significance and distinguish between non-negotiable issues and those that can be addressed through repairs, credits, or price adjustments. Act promptly to complete agreed-upon repairs, ensuring a positive experience for all parties involved and setting the stage for a smooth closing. This section aims to provide the insights needed to navigate the inspection process confidently as a seller, contributing to a constructive real estate transaction.

Navigating the Appraisal Process

Once you've made it through inspections, being prepared for the appraisal process is essential. An appraisal is an independent assessment of your property's value conducted by a licensed appraiser, and lenders rely on appraisals to ensure that the property's value aligns with the loan amount.

During the appraisal process, presenting your inherited estate in the best possible light is crucial. Showcase recent improvements or renovations and be open to discussions with the appraiser, providing any relevant information that could influence their assessment.

If the appraisal comes in lower than the agreed upon purchase price then the buyer and seller will have to come together to find a solution whether that be lowering the purchase price, having the buyer bring more cash to the table, rebutting the appraisal, or terminating the purchase agreement altogether if a solution can not be made.

If you're listing with a realtor, they will guide you through the appraisal process and assist with reassessing the pricing strategy if needed. Realtors bring a wealth of experience in navigating every aspect of the selling process, allowing sellers to focus on making informed decisions while confidently moving toward a successful sale.

Finalizing the Deal

Once negotiations reach a favorable outcome, and any changes to the purchase agreement are made, your next stop will be the closing table. Sellers should remain diligent during this phase, ensuring that all terms are accurately reflected in the contract. Realtors guide sellers through this process, ensuring a seamless transition towards closing. They take care of the detailed paperwork, legal aspects, and finalization of the deal, allowing sellers to focus on the successful culmination of the transaction.

In the subsequent chapters, we'll dive into the closing process, including the finalization of legal and financial details. Understanding the art of negotiations positions sellers for success, allowing them to navigate this pivotal phase with confidence and achieve a mutually beneficial agreement for both them and the buyer.

* * *

Chapter 9 Summary:

Understanding the Buyer's Perspective

- Recognize that buyers seek value and may scrutinize aspects for negotiation.
- Anticipate potential negotiation points by considering the buyer's motivations.
- The realtor plays a crucial role in deciphering and addressing buyer motivations.

Expectations and Flexibility

- Set realistic expectations grounded in market realities.
- Balance financial goals with market conditions, guided by the realtor's expertise.
- Flexibility is valuable; be open to compromises for a smoother negotiation process.

Realtor's Role in Negotiations

- The realtor serves as a crucial ally, assessing offers and

providing strategic advice.
- Guides sellers on market dynamics, buyer behavior, and balancing assertiveness with flexibility.

Patience in Negotiations

- Negotiations can be time-consuming; exercise patience for thoughtful consideration.
- Realtors manage timelines to ensure efficient and effective negotiation progress.

Navigating the Inspection Process as a Seller

- Address issues proactively based on earlier evaluations or recommendations.
- Allow space for the buyer and inspector during the inspection without interference.

Handling Inspection Findings

- Expect a detailed report outlining structural, system, and appliance findings.
- Collaboratively approach negotiations based on reasonable buyer concerns.

Prompt Action on Agreed Repairs

- Prioritize repairs based on significance and promptly address agreed-upon repairs.
- Foster a positive experience for all parties involved, contributing to a smooth closing.

Navigating the Appraisal Process

- Showcase recent improvements and renovations during the appraisal.
- Be open to discussions with the appraiser, providing relevant information.

Realtor's Guidance in Appraisal

- Realtors guide sellers through the appraisal process and reassess pricing strategies.
- Utilize the realtor's experience to navigate every aspect of the selling process.

Finalizing the Deal

- Ensure accurate representation of all terms in the purchase agreement.
- Realtors handle detailed paperwork, legal aspects, and finalize the deal for a seamless transition.

10

Navigating Legalities and Finalizing the Transaction

As negotiations culminate in a mutually agreeable arrangement, the focus shifts to the final stages of the selling process. Closing the deal involves navigating legalities, ensuring financial clarity, and executing a seamless transfer of ownership. In this chapter, we delve into the details of finalizing the transaction, providing an understanding of the steps involved.

The legalities of closing a real estate deal are multifaceted and require the seller's attention. Sellers must ensure that all necessary legal documents are in order to facilitate a smooth transition of ownership. This usually includes the deed, which verifies ownership rights, and the purchase agreement, which outlines the terms agreed upon during negotiations. Collaborating closely with a real estate attorney or title company and realtor is crucial at this stage. They play a pivotal role in reviewing and preparing the necessary legal documents, ensuring compliance with local regulations, and addressing any potential issues that may arise during the process.

Closing also involves a comprehensive examination of financial details to ensure clarity and transparency. Sellers must be prepared to settle any outstanding debts or liens on the property, ensuring a clean transfer of ownership. Additionally, both parties need to understand the closing costs, which encompass various fees such as property taxes, legal fees, and real estate agent commissions. This will be outlined on the settlement statement.

The settlement statement is a detailed breakdown of the financial aspects of the transaction, and is a key document in this phase. Collaborating with a realtor and financial advisor can be beneficial at this step. They provide insights into the financial implications of the deal, helping sellers understand closing costs and ensuring a financially sound conclusion.

In the period leading up to closing, any agreed-upon repairs or conditions must be fulfilled. Home inspections may have revealed certain issues that need attention, and sellers are responsible for ensuring these are addressed before the finalization of the deal. This involves coordinating with contractors, providing documentation of completed repairs, and ensuring that the property meets the agreed-upon standards.

A closing agent, often an escrow officer or real estate attorney, is a third party responsible for orchestrating the final stages of the transaction. They play an important role in ensuring that all the necessary documents are signed, funds are appropriately disbursed, and the transfer of ownership is executed smoothly. Sellers can rely on the expertise of the closing agent to guide them through the closing process, answering any questions and addressing concerns that may arise. The closing agent acts as a central figure in coordinating the efforts of all parties involved, fostering a collaborative environment that contributes to the overall success of the transaction.

Transferring Utilities and Closing Day Preparations

In the days leading up to closing, sellers need to coordinate the transfer of utilities to the buyer. This involves notifying utility companies of the impending ownership transfer and ensuring a seamless transition of services. Additionally, sellers should prepare for the closing day by having all necessary documents and keys ready. Collaborating closely with the realtor and closing agent is essential during this phase. They provide guidance on the logistics of the handover, ensuring that the property is presented in its agreed-upon condition, and all necessary items are in place for the buyer to assume ownership seamlessly.

It is common in real estate transactions that the buyers will want to walk through the property a few days prior to close to ensure that the property is in the agreed-upon condition. This is called a "final walkthrough" and is typically outlined in the purchase agreement.

Post-Closing Considerations

Once the transaction is complete, and ownership has officially transferred to the buyer, it's time to celebrate the successful transition. Sellers can take a moment to reflect on the entire selling process, acknowledging the efforts invested and the positive outcome achieved. Realtors may continue to offer support during this post-closing phase, providing guidance on any lingering questions or considerations that may arise. Sellers can confidently move forward, knowing that they have navigated the complexities of selling an inherited estate with diligence and expertise.

In the final chapter, we'll explore considerations for sellers after the closing, including reflections on the selling experience, potential next steps, and the lasting impact of successfully navigating the real estate transaction. Understanding the nuances of closing the deal positions sellers for a smooth transition and a positive outcome at the conclusion of their real estate journey.

Pro Tip: Closing Day Essentials

Prepare a closing day essentials kit, including all relevant documents, keys, and any necessary information for a seamless handover. Having everything organized and readily accessible reduces stress on the closing day and ensures a smooth transition of ownership.

* * *

Chapter 10 Summary:

Legalities of Closing

- Ensure necessary legal documents, including the title deed and purchase agreement, are in order.

- Collaborate with a real estate attorney, title company, and realtor to navigate legal aspects and address issues.
- Safeguard the integrity of the transaction by adhering to local regulations.

Financial Examination

- Settle outstanding debts or liens on the property for a clean transfer of ownership.
- Understand and address closing costs, encompassing property taxes, legal fees, and agent commissions.
- Utilize the Settlement Statement for a detailed breakdown of financial aspects with guidance from a realtor and financial advisor.

Fulfilling Agreed-upon Conditions

- Complete any repairs or conditions agreed upon before closing.
- Realtors facilitate communication between parties, ensuring stipulated conditions are met to satisfaction.

Role of the Closing Agent

- A closing agent, often an escrow officer or real estate attorney, orchestrates the final stages of the transaction.
- Ensures all necessary documents are signed, funds are disbursed appropriately, and ownership transfer is smooth.

- Acts as a central figure in coordinating efforts, fostering a collaborative environment.

Transferring Utilities and Closing Day Preparations

- Coordinate the transfer of utilities to the buyer leading up to closing.
- Prepare for closing day with necessary documents and keys in collaboration with the realtor and closing agent.
- Final walkthrough ensures the property is in the agreed-upon condition before close.

Post-Closing Considerations

- Reflect on the selling process and acknowledge positive outcomes.
- Realtors offer continued support in addressing lingering questions or considerations.
- Sellers confidently move forward, having navigated the complexities of selling an inherited estate diligently.

11

Moving Forward: Transitioning to a New Chapter

As the final ink dries on the closing documents and the keys are handed over to the new owners, sellers embark on a reflective phase of the real estate journey. Let's discuss post-closing considerations, reflections on the selling experience, potential next steps, and the lasting impact of successfully navigating the real estate transaction.

Take a moment to reflect on the entire selling experience. Consider the lessons learned, challenges overcome, and the achievements attained. Reflecting on the selling process allows sellers to gain valuable insights into their own preferences, priorities, and the dynamics of the real estate market. This self-awareness becomes a foundation for future endeavors, whether they involve additional real estate transactions or other life pursuits.

Sellers should assess the financial outcomes of the transaction. Evaluate the net proceeds from the sale, considering factors such as closing costs, outstanding mortgage balances, and any negotiated repairs or concessions. Understanding the financial bottom line provides clarity on the overall success of the transaction and informs future financial decisions.

Emotional Closure

Selling an inherited estate often carries emotional weight. Take the time to navigate the personal impact of parting with a property that may hold sentimental value. Embrace the positive aspects of the transition, acknowledging that the property will now have the opportunity to create new memories for its new owners. Seek emotional closure by focusing on the positive aspects of the selling experience and the possibilities that lie ahead.

Impact on Estate Planning: Reassessing Your Overall Strategy

The successful sale of an inherited estate may prompt a reassessment of your overall estate planning strategy. Consult with legal and financial professionals to ensure that your estate plan aligns with your current circumstances and future goals. This may involve updating wills, trusts, or beneficiary designations to reflect changes in your assets and priorities.

Philanthropic Considerations

If the inherited estate held significant value, consider philan-thropic contributions as part of your post-closing considera-tions. Explore opportunities to give back to the community or support causes that align with your values. Philanthropy can be a meaningful way to leverage the financial success of the real estate transaction for the greater good.

In concluding this book, the journey of selling an inherited estate is not just a financial transaction but an experience that encompasses emotional, personal, and strategic considerations. By navigating each phase thoughtfully and collaboratively, sellers position themselves for a successful outcome and set the stage for positive future real estate endeavors. The impact of successfully selling an inherited estate extends beyond the closing table, leaving sellers with valuable lessons, financial clarity, and a sense of accomplishment.

Take the time to reflect on your values and priorities. The sale of an inherited estate can prompt a reassessment of what truly matters to you. Consider aligning your life choices with your values, whether it involves spending more time with family, contributing to charitable causes, or embracing a lifestyle that reflects your core principles. This introspective process ensures that your decisions align with your authentic self.